Blindsided

Also by Jack Myers

BLINDSIDED

Poems by
JACK MYERS

DAVID R. GODINE, PUBLISHER, BOSTON

First edition published in 1993 by
David R. Godine, Publisher, Inc.
Horticultural Hall
300 Massachusetts Avenue
Boston, Massachusetts 02115 .

The publisher acknowledges the copyright holders for the following poems:
"Visitation Rites," *Poetry,* June 1988, © The Modern Poetry Association;
"The BamButti: Pygmies of the Congo," *The Kenyon Review,* Spring 1990,
© The Kenyon Review; "How?" *The Kenyon Review,* Summer 1990, © The
Kenyon Review.

Library of Congress Cataloguing-in-Publication Data
Myers, Jack Elliott, 1941–
Blindsided : poems / by Jack Myers.–1st ed.
p. cm.
ISBN 0-87923-956-5
I. Title.
PS3563.Y42B64 1993 92-39479
811'.54—dc20 CIP

First edition
Printed in the United States of America

The author wishes to thank the following journals in which some of the poems in this book first appeared:

The American Poetry Review	The Experts
Balcones	Jake Addresses the World from the Garden
Chadakoin Review	Vanishing Days; Talking to Arthur
Colorado North Review	The Amazing Obsolete TV Magnifying Viewer
The Contemporary Review	Looking at Death Through Bad Eyes; The Stopover Not Thinking of Himself; I Told You So Sometimes, Sweetie, You Think Too Much Please, Not All at Once
Crazy Horse	The Energy It Takes to Pass Through Solid Objects; Washed Up
Denver Quarterly	The Wild and Real Agency Beating Back Death with a Lilac Bush
The Eleventh Muse	The Inner Life; What's the Difference?; On Refusing
The Great River Review	A Living; 100%; Gifts That Get Lost One, Two, Three, Four, Five . . .
Green Mountains Review	The Underwater River
The Kenyon Review	How?; The BamButti: Pygmies of the Congo
The Missouri Review	I Don't Know, You Know Everything I Know Why Don't You Ask Your Father?
New Myths: MSS.	Blockbuster; The Man of Steel
The North American Review	Have A Nice Day
Poetry	Visitation Rites
Poetry East	The Aesthetes
Southwest Review	From the Luxury Condo on the Sea
The Taos Review	Excuse Me; Supersaver to Atlanta; Convention
Willow Springs	Attack of the Killer Power Tools; Alien

The author also wishes to gratefully acknowledge the National Endowment for the Arts and Southern Methodist University whose generous fellowships helped make a number of these poems possible.

Thanks also to Mark Cox, Leslie Ullman, Peter Feldman, Tony Hoagland, and Ralph Angel for the generosity of their critical commentaries on this manuscript.

For my children, Ben, Seth, Jake, and Jessie

Contents

But it is not so easy to tell you about Anna Ignatievna.
First of all, I know almost nothing about her, and secondly,
I have just fallen off my chair and forget what I was going
to say. So I better tell you about myself.

—DANIIL KHARMS
"Symphony No. 2"

Blindsided

Jake Addresses the World from the Garden

> Rocks without ch'i [spirit] are dead rocks.
> — MAI-MAI SZE, *The Way of Chinese Painting*

It's spring and Jake toddles to the garden
as the sun wobbles up clean and iridescent.

He points to the stones asleep and says, "M'mba,"
I guess for the sound they make, takes another step

and says, "M'mba," for the small red berries crying
in the holly. "M'mba" for the first sweet sadness

of the purplish-black berries in the drooping monkey grass,
and "M'mba," for the little witches' faces bursting into blossom.

That's what it's like being shorter than the primary colors,
being deafened by humming stones while the whole world billows

behind the curtain "M'mba," the one word. Meanwhile I go on
troweling, slavering the world with language as Jake squeals

like a held bird and begins lallalating to me in tongues.
I follow him around as he tries to thread the shine off a stone

through the eye of a watchful bird. After a year of banging
his head, all the crying, the awful falling down, now he's trying

to explain the vast brightening in his brain by saying "M'mba"
to me again and again. And though I follow with the sadness

above which a stone cannot lift itself, I wink and say
"M'mba" back to him. But I don't mean it.

Visitation Rites

for my son Seth

My gentle son is performing tricks for me on his bicycle.
He's fourteen and has just cracked open the storm door
to manhood with his gently lowered voice shredding
into shadows until he's surrounded by the calls of
tan young girls whose smooth brown skin calls out, "We're alone."

It will not be long before he masters standing still
on one wheel, elegant jumps over obstacles, riding
upside down and backward until he will have made
of danger a pretty colored bird to delight him,
sending it away, calling it home, calling it home
as it sails and grows larger, darkens and adds weight.

I watch how well he has done without me all these years,
me with my iron sled of guilt, my cooked-out piles of
worry smoldering. I have been his only model, he says,
and shares with me what a typical day of winning is like.
I sit on a little hill watching my son show off his
light dominion over gravity, knowing in the next few minutes

I will leave again for another year, and again our lives
will pull apart and heal over like bubbles separating in two.
This is how he says good-bye — without speech or reasons or
the long looking after that I have honed through time —
just in a flash in the sun he's suddenly perfected, and I'm gone.

4

Have a Nice Day

No, no, I don't want my heart broken again today.
I don't want to hear the slosh and slide of another country-
western tune about bars and broken-down love and junky pickups,
though they're more than real enough. And I don't want to feel
the sentimental night sweats rising up from someone's childhood,
or tangle with the slashes of abstract art drying in the track-lit air
of grown-up feelings, watching the colors of memory and fact intersect
and crash like trucks, as if thought were feeling, and feelings, trucks.

I just want what we used to wish for back in the 1950s, to have
"a nice day," back when a woman would seriously ask without blinking,
"If I take off all my clothes, will you take care of me the rest of my life?"
Back when most of the guys I knew would've given this serious thought,
though it all seems sort of silly now, almost heartbreakingly incompetent
in its innocence, in its presumption of real loss, like the guys
elbowing each other on the corner, asking "How far did you get?" as if
the body, like the expression "nice," were a place you could retire to.

Everyone's suffered real losses, which means there is no "far enough."
And I don't want to harken back to yesteryear when being good or bad
was the simple difference between an open heart (now a surgical procedure)
and a closed door (signifying power), back when work was poetically called
"earning a living," as if merely living weren't work enough.
Everyone seems headed for his own compulsory heart attack, proving, yes,
the heart has gone far enough. And I'm not sure what's coming next

though yesterday I saw some kids with Day-Glo hair and death heads
on their teeth. They were sloppily slam-dancing on ice, which was just
their way of probably saying yes, we're broken-hearted, without taking
their clothes off. That seems more than hard enough. Today I just want
to relax, bring my blood pressure down to the level of rush-hour traffic.
I suppose that makes me as outdated as this tree I'm sitting under,

on whose every leaf is a black-eyed, green-bellied cicada buzz-sawing
its wire-and-cellophane grade school wings in the last-chance blood lust
of August. They seem willing and able to leave the burning husks
of their bodies behind in the trees, as I seem to be doing,
for the sake of a kind word.

Not Thinking of Himself

for Mark Cox

"Today," he said to the mirror, "the person I am inside of
will not be allowed to think of himself. Not once!"

And immediately he smashed his toe on the corner of the sink
but thought only of his mother who used to pinch his cheeks
like this—"Ow!"—and crush his chest like that—"Ow!"

He wondered briefly if under his rules it would be allowable
to do something nice for someone who didn't know he existed.

And immediately he stood up and banged his head on the water tank
but thought only of his father who used to hit him on the head
like this—"Ow!"—and punch him in the chest like that—"Ow!"

It was then that he thought of his life as an inside-out sock,
and wondered briefly if calling himself by another name completely
might give him a bigger head start.

The Experts

When the man in the window seat
flying next to me
asks me who I am
and I tell him I'm a poet,
he turns embarrassed toward the sun.
The woman on the other side of me
pipes up she's four-foot-ten and is going to sue
whoever made these seats.

And so it is I'm reminded how I wish I were
one of the aesthetes
floating down double-lit canals
of quiet listening, the ones
who come to know something as
mysterious and useless
as when a tree has decided to sleep.

You would think for them
pain lights up the edges of everything,
burns right through the center of every leaf,
but I've seen them strolling around,
their faces glistening with the sort of peace
only sleep can polish babies with.

And so when a waitress in San Antonio
asks me what I do, and I think
how the one small thing I've learned
seems more complex the more I think of it,
how the joys of it have overpowered me
long after I don't understand,

I tell her "Corned beef on rye, a side of salad,
hold the pickle, I'm a poet," and she stops to talk

about her little son who, she says, can hurt himself
even when he's sitting still. I tell her
there's a poem in that, and she repeats
"Hold the pickle, I'm a poet,"
then looks at me and says, "I know."

How?

The fat lady behind the counter at the gas station
wore a pin that said, "I've lost 15 lbs. Ask me how!"
That was answered by the vision of her daughter,
obviously being punished, bent over a book in the corner,
like a Vermeer in reverse.

Then it struck me how that girl, quietly displayed there,
was like her mother's button, and I wanted to ask her how.
But her mother snapped a few bills into my extended hand,
saying, "Have a nice day," meaning, mind my own business.

I guess I half-expected the daughter to flash me a desperate look,
like in the movies where the mirror in the ladies' room
is scrawled in blood, "I've lost 15 lbs. Ask me how!"
But she never gave me the slightest look.

And as I pounded the car across the compressor hose, I knew that
in the movie I would've leapt from the swerving car and crashed
headfirst through the complacency of their plate glass window
where they pretended to be the perfect picture of the average

alienated American family, with Dad out back under a car,
and I'd put a gun to her fat mother's head and nonchalantly say,
"Okay, Baby Shoes, unless you want to lose another 15 lbs.,
you better tell me how, and tell it to me slowly."

Only in real life I just drove on,
swerving toward the "before picture" of the daughter,
surprised at how far out of myself I had gone,
blindsided by the "after picture" of her mother,
who pinned me under the wreckage of some incomprehensible sadness,
making me check and recheck my change.

The Wild and Real Agency

Once I took my wife against her will
to a modeling studio, helped her change
into dozens of compelling women, took her
down the long corridor of self-doubt
to a flood-lit room where she stood alone
against a pulled-down sky of blue.

The owner, who was secretly going out of business,
kept urging the ultimate woman out of her,
the way rock stars struggle toward their scream:
"Lemme have a little more. More pout. I need
that sadness, Baby. Now lemme have more leg."

That interested me when we first got married,
the dance behind the dance, but "The last thing
that is coming out of me," she said, "is me."
"Perfect, Babe," he said looking at her upside down
from beneath his black hood, and the flashbulbs
went off like fast days passing.

Then a real model came in complaining about her work.
She made this business of phony pleasure an object of belief,
and we felt foolish, my wife half-undressed, and me
caught with the next change of costume frozen in my head.

I guess it was that sense of cheapness and the opportunity
to escape that created an aura of beautiful importance between us,
like lovers in foreign films, as if the heart
had gained its final coup through an ordinary distraction,
or maybe Beauty herself decided it was time to show us her

surreal leg. "Who goes to a mall to be famous?" my wife said
as we drove home with the windows down, thrilled there was
real weather, taking the curves in slowly, and my wife
stretched back in her faded jeans looking really beautiful.

Why Don't You Ask Your Father?

Action is so epigrammatic, discharging its meaning like a joke.
Every deed is a loss of consciousness; every act is a black-out.
— JOHN HOLLANDER, *Translation from the French*

After I bought our little kiddie pool and set it up,
I realized I had placed it under an overhang without a gutter,
and, of course, the weatherman called for rain. And so
I scrounged around the house for stuff to make a cover

and, for height, I used our old director's chairs,
the ones we sit in when we argue, which we got for showing up
at a time-share place in Arkansas and announced on cue,
"We only want the gift!"

Then to smooth that out I placed a plastic laundry basket
upside down on top of them, the one that wrenched my back
just before my fatal trip to meet your mother who laid me out
all week in her guest room for the dead, and then

I jerry-rigged my painter's tarp across that, the one
that I salvaged from my one and only business, and stretched it
taut across some wires I broke off from the tomato cages,
in which you mistakenly grew decorative pickle dwarfs,

and fitted them together with some duct tape I had borrowed
from my neighbor who has five kids and no hope and no job
and then placed the fragile top across the tottering platform
of the laundry basket and then carefully sliced open

our old prenuptial water bed, which was always cold and
rolly anyway, and plunked that down on top of everything
so it wouldn't all blow away, and then I built a runway
from the garden timbers I ripped off from the railroad yard

where we had our first romantic encounter and ran those suckers
straight out across the yard and under the fence and out to

the city gutter. I've found that like me everything has
a use opposite to its intended. And then I slammed on

my old Nor'easter hat and matching yellow slicker,
which I kept from my fiscally pitiful lobstering days,
and with my kids jumping up and down crying "Daddy! Daddy!"
in the window, I sat there by the pool waiting for the
rain—it goddamn better rain—to come.

 Alien

How is it I often find myself
standing here, spinning in my head
like a Rolodex of addresses,
as if I've stopped outside
the house that I grew up in,
and am afraid to go in?

When I was beaten and kicked by ten men,
everywhere I threw a punch it landed.
It was all adrenaline,
a gorgeous, heady light.

But it was the obliviousness of it
that I liked, like when I'm yelling
at my wife because I'm mad at someone else
and she says, "Look at your face! Alien!"

Maybe those guys were mad at me
for walking naked and drunk out of a moonlit pool
in front of their screaming crinoline dates
when all I was doing was being me
without knowing it.

The day after I got punched out
and went back, I discovered a shotgun pattern
of head-size holes in the wall,
but I couldn't remember any of it.

I thought that kind of being by myself
must have been marvelous,
and suddenly I wanted my life to be like
one long series of violent misses,
and for a long time
I stood there by myself.

The Inner Life

for Gordon Weaver

5 A.M. and the baby is rolling back and forth between us singing,
"Kiss the Mommy, kiss the Daddy, kiss the Mommy, kiss the Daddy,"
and five hours later I slip into the towering university where
Prof. Garhart declares, "Hark! There's a poet among us!" then
laughs like a clock, "Har. Har. Har. Har." and I feel dizzy
like I'm walking on deep sponge cake and my fifth demitasse of
aqua vitae has decided to become a screwdriver, making me epiphanize
how poetry is just like life when the phone rings and, yes, I will
be happy to appear for nothing, I was born wasn't I, and I go
to teach Great Literature and on the way I'm trying to retrieve
my idea of why I thought life was like poetry when one of my students
rounding the corner catches me absentmindedly picking my nose
just as I think I have it.

On Refusing Gifts That Get Lost

after Po Chu-i

When I bought my wife gold earrings for her birthday,
I pictured them flashing in her black hair, thrilling me a little
like in the old days, like a glimpse of thigh inside a skirt.

It was around then that I read in the newspaper that anyone
who gets angry six or seven times a day has a real problem.
I already knew that about myself, but still, coming like that
in the form of a public announcement, it was a bit of a shock.

But last night, just before her birthday, my wife looked closely
into my eyes, like she always does when she wants the real dirt,
and said: "Darling, the only thing I have ever lost on this earth
are earrings. You better show me what you bought."

That's why I'm standing here in line undoing what I wanted
yesterday, hissing at the formidable Refund Lady that I'm next,
that all I've ever done is wait, that I'm getting old and ugly,
and that I demand to speak to the person in charge about this.

Only the lovely Giftwrap Girl, smearing my anger with her smile,
understands this: "No, no," she says, "these earrings wouldn't be right
for your wife. They're for someone young and full of life," she smiles,
"someone like me!" Then she resmiles very excellently.

The Amazing Obsolete TV Magnifying Viewer

What a disappointment, like looking through the end of a Coke bottle
at *The Ed Sullivan Show*, its lurid edges glowing all the way
to the spare bedroom where Aunt Jenny, once the class act of the family
in her svelte black dresses and gold jewelry, now blind in one eye
from hardening of the arteries, sat wheezing on the edge of the bed
from emphysema in her blowsy bathrobe and pink bunny slippers,
examining the identical cleaved halves of her migraine headache.

In those days the juggling acts always seemed so stupid,
whole extended families of Slavs brought in for a command performance:
mothers, fathers, uncles, children all standing on top of each other's
shoulders, all rocking madly on a teeter-totter board
to the music of the Russian kazatsky, while torches and swords
flew like family arguments up and down the human ladder.

I had just turned thirteen and was the family's self-appointed critic.
I sat a room away sniping at the rotten talent while the family,
without looking back at me, dismissed my running commentary
with an exasperated, "Oh, Jackie!" meaning I couldn't spot a metaphor
if it were burned onto a stage with sweeping spotlights.

And it was true. All I was doing was erasing the past as it ran,
though it all seems sharp as a subpoena, with me the hostile witness
screaming offstage, "Heresay! Heresay!" while the family flickered,
disbanded, some going mad, the rest "dying from fatal diseases."

All the while things in my head kept getting blurrier and bigger,
like the amazing obsolete TV magnifying viewer whose dot of light
diminished as I forgot it all—the house with its furor and heartaches
demolished, and me, still sitting there in the formal living room,
a room away, watching the family amazed at the juggling acts,
ooing and ahhing, and me, waiting to grow up, just waiting.

Attack of the Killer Power Tools

The whine of a circular saw
flew around the house today
like the prehistoric mating call
of some zinc-voiced mutant insect.
It came cornering this way,
clean as a right angle
spewing a snowstorm of decisions
I just couldn't put my finger on.

I felt like the studio violinist
who stayed home practicing
his entire childhood,
sawing his way through
facsimiles of the classics,
and turned out to be
a studio violinist.

So I painted the kitchen cabinets
with what turned out to be
a garish semigloss blue
like the horses on the merry-go-round
rearing up from what I took to be
a relentless electrical shock
while the world went round and round.

That's when my wife came in screaming
"Stop this kitchen now!"
which slowed my enthusiasm down
to a thousand-pound vowel,
which felt like I was standing
on my own sad song

about the little bald man
in the fluorescent hardware store
vowing to me this color
was true Renaissance blue.

I felt as if I had been holding a violin
under my chin for years, which reminded me
of my appointment at the dentist
who lectures me until my mouth is numb
though he lets me put the pedal of his drill
to the floor while he goes over and over
the smallest details until I feel at home
inside the bad art on his wall.

All this practicing of distractions
and crossed-out mistakes makes me think
I could be the Jackson Pollock of my life,
and I could scribble that out too,
if I had a mind to.
Only once in a while I stand back
from my life and think
there must be a power tool for this.

Symphony No. 2

Ah, milk,
that'll do the trick,
he thinks, as he pours it over his cereal

and baby slams her head
and screams rounding the corner
and son is whining on the couch
his Mutant Ninja Turtle show is over.

Father forces the cereal under the milk,
scoops the milk back over,
over and under, back and forth
until they're properly mixed.

That ought to hold him till lunch,
he thinks. "What's for lunch?"
he asks the wife

who bruises past him
complaining how he kneed and elbowed her,
hogged the blankets, talked all night in his sleep,
the pig.

"Honey! What's for lunch!?"

Vanishing Days

When I was a child
I ran and leapt along the beach
until I was made of
the striking power of wind.

I swam out and dove beneath
the cold blue water
and did somersaults
until I felt beautiful like water.

And when I wrote, first I lost
my right hand, then both arms,
and when I came to an understanding
only a ring spread out where I was.

I suppose I will go on doing this
to feel the impossibly huge things
of this world pass through me
as if I were missing. To live fully,
you must have a perfect disguise.

The Man of Steel

for Albert Goldbarth

Screeching up to me, up to my waist, little Jake,
disguised in a mild-mannered towel, asks frantically,
"Can I save you, Dad?" He's got that hysterical gleam
in his eye, meaning something's up, things have gone awry,
and since I'm just another hapless victim in the universe,
I accede and admit, "Help me, I'm falling."

So on he climbs atop the kitchen table, straddles
the eggs, snaps open his towel and reveals
the Man of Steel, complete in sky-blue pajamas and
screaming red cape, and proclaims in Kryptonic Capital Letters:
"I WILL SAVE YOU, DAD!" Then down he jumps
and, with eyes scrinched shut in intergalactic penetration,
he holds me and makes that whizzing sound, "Sssssst . . . ,"
that means he's flying me back to safety where I am.

I believe in a blithering sweet nothingness
in the coming afterlife, and in this one
only the little blue headlong man who saves me
from myself, then dives off to reverse other disasters:
a fire that started as a living room magically blooms
into a living room again; "YOW!-YOW!-YOW!" his X-ray vision
zaps the evil genius, Dr. Zebart, leaving a dead fly
on the windowsill sizzling deader still; then "Zsssssst!"
he freezes a maverick planet in its place and restores
the music of the spheres back to its windless space.

But even as the Man of Steel sleeps, he knows everything normal
around him will continue to sink and fray and untwist. I believe
in the happy ending of the ten acrylic suns shining on his fingertips,
how they foretell of a never-known millennium of peace.
But only the Man of Steel in his wisdom knows that first
it will be brought on by a series of natural disasters
of somewhat suspicious origins.

I Told You So

Anyway, she said if and when they ever got married
they would have to have at least two kids and
maybe as many as six.
And if they weren't getting married,
well, adios love-of-my-life, those are the rules,
hurry up, take it or leave it, this is my life.

Anyway, for many years after they were married
she kept pestering him not to do this and not to do that
and, most of all, to stop smoking. In other words,
each year she turned the key in his back
another 365 notches
until, finally, unable to laugh without coughing,
and having to suffer those I-told-you-so looks of hers
in the midst of one of these fits, he made himself quit.

But as the smoke cleared out of his lungs,
each day he filled up with more and more anger until
he would explode on a moment's notice like this:
"Hey! Turn the heat up when you're making sizzling *fajitas*!
I want to see that pan glow red!" He wanted to hear
the hysterical crackling and watch the frenzied dance
of the water-dot extinguishing itself across the pan.

He remembered getting that pan from a stern Amish man
dressed in black, a man who seemed mad at him for no reason.
Maybe the pan was cursed. Who knows, anyway he yelled,
"You don't wash a pan like that in water! You heat it up
until it sizzles, and you look around the house
thinking, 'Hmmm, things are getting a little crazy,'
until a little voice inside you starts to say
'I told you so.'"

Anyway, one day when he couldn't stand himself any longer
he yelled at her and she splattered her arms with
boiling hot grease and screamed like one of those
little police whistles with the dried pea in it,
and he screamed at the baby who was crying, and then
everybody closed their eyes and screamed, "I told you so!"

Anyway, after they came home from the hospital,
very tired, very scared, very sorry, and a lot poorer,
they promised they would never do that again,
and the next day he came out of the shower
and announced a new rule: There would be no more
frying in hot oil, especially in anger,
and only two more children, goddammit.
To hell with that shit.

Sometimes, Sweetie, You Think Too Much

When he wanted to tell her
something important,
he'd get a big feeling
like a dumpster being lifted
over the front end of his face.

And just as he was about to
unload, she'd say something
little-and-sweet and beside-the-point
and he'd end up in a fit
of random air brakes.

When he'd wake up in the morning,
looking like he just came home from work,
he'd intone, "I have a terrible grief to tell . . ."

and she'd look into the faces of
her chipped toenails and sort of
half-warn, half-sing,
"Oh, hootie, tootie, mootie, smootie, rootie . . ."

Blockbuster

I used to love to stalk the dimly lit bookstalls in Harvard Square,
agonizing over my tremulous choice of a book, each thin volume
a meal I'd live on for a week, my blind date, my shotgun marriage,
my wild and hungry progeny. And if it were quicklime and anchovies
or a rope of garlic and hot peppers, then that's what I ate,
and that's how I lived, and that's how I dreamt.

But now I'm gliding through the new boutiques and flashy franchises
of Dallas, sliding along the glossy shelves like Catherine the Great
of Russia, reviewing the booming stalls of her nightly lovers in 1796,
when the ropes of her lust exploded and she got crushed by a horse.

That's where I found myself last night, hoisting a complimentary copy
of *The Norton Anthology* above my bed, opening my mind's mouth wide,
my mind's ear wide, all my pickled senses, hoping I'd get hurt.
And when I was engorged and overawed and dead and emptied out like Jo

I found myself back sleeping it off in my old garage, writing my way
inward inside my faithfully ticking Chevy that had wings of chrome,
balding tires, a smell of dust like the life of the mind, 150,000 miles,
and was so broken in it could take itself for a ride.

Give me back my attic with its little childhood window and the light
that swung above my head like hunger. You can take my ox-blood scarf,
my daring acrylic satchel, and the ruby from my engorged pinkie.
Tell me how I've lost my way, how I'm an insult to my old ambition,

because the way things are going now all the books seem ghosted
by some disembodied hand on self-consuming paper, and I'm getting strar
I'm getting louder, I'm getting stronger, and I swear to whatever's left
that's holy, I'll cut off the hands of anyone who gets in my way.

The Æsthetes

for Ruth Greene

I know there are a lucky few out there
alone and still
like Northern trees
who watch the green and red and yellow
tearing from the faces of the leaves,
who let their faces blow away
and the self fall through
a twilit space of magenta wandering.

How does it feel to be bare and lit,
not to have to close your eyes
to refresh the mind's reception,
not to fall on a bed that opens
onto dark atomic weather,
but listening as easily as
breathing colors skin, deftly touching
each new smallness as it rises into everything?

Isn't that the way to see, looking up
with a face that doesn't know it's there,
letting it rise and elongate and mirror
the bottom of every falling raindrop
and on that day look up and say
it's not me, it's raining.
And maybe it won't even be raining,
but will be me,
walking over the newfound freedom
of the leaves, feeling everything.

⌐ Washed Up

When the flyweight
who was just a skinny kid
with the snappy moniker,
"*La Cucaracha*," went down
in the first round
from a short right cross
my sister could've taken,
it was pretty obvious
he didn't want to box.
He wanted out.
He just sat there
busted up, twice defeated
in two pro fights,
his pipe-stem arms
dangling through the ropes,
his head slung down
as if he were enduring
another hellish argument
at home, the gulps of light
from hungry reporters
ripping into him
like his father
screaming, "Get a job!"

It was funny at first
seeing him sink down,
legs splayed like a girl's,
like your little sister's,
counting her defeat
her best escape.
Then it was sad
'cause you could see
he didn't have the heart,

that he was only waiting
for someone to help him up,
tell him, "It's okay, kid, go home."
Then it was kind of quiet,
kind of scary as we began to relate,
like watching the dead
grow hair and nails,
and still no one came.

Oh well, we thought,
trying to change the subject,
what's next?
But the camera stayed on him,
coldly telling us
what to think,
while the kid couldn't
figure out how to get
his mouthpiece out.
It was as if he had discovered
some huge foreign thing
in his mouth, like in the
beginning of a horror movie,
when his hand couldn't grasp
this glistening red mass,
couldn't gasp or cough it up.
What's next? we wondered,
gently turning to one another
as men seldom do, our minds
flexed for the punchline
of a joke.
But when we turned back
the kid was gone
and somebody's sister

was flung over the hood
of a new red sports car
and that was that.

And I forgot about the kid
until this morning
when I was watching a
dingy gray sea gull
walking along, poking at the
receding shoreline and thinking
how stupid it is
just to settle for whatever
is accidentally washed up
when there're millions of square miles
of ocean lying unconscious
next to him, if he'd just lift his head.
The whole thing seemed like
some huge and subtle screening process
I just couldn't figure out,
like someone who's been
on the road too long
not being in control of where
or when he sleeps. It was like

coming out of a movie
into the roaring light of a day
you had forgotten
and being faced with
seeing everything finally
for what it is. I don't know—
the sea, the fight, the clichéd
story of his life —
maybe it was just a case of

selective perception
and later on
inside some woman that night
he'd pull out and it'd all seem
like a case of mistaken identity.

I don't know,
I used to like the fights,
the edgy waiting, the thrill
of knocking someone out,
the fists, the muscle, the shouts.
Now I mostly hear the body punches slamming home,
the twisting of the turnbuckles.
All of a sudden
I feel what it's like
to be hooked in the mouth
and pulled up into a life
not your own,
the kid with a name
that doesn't fit,
beaten up, craning his neck around
to see what he's missed,
getting to his knees,
confused and humiliated,
swearing he can keep on
taking it
if that's what they want,
if that's what it takes,
if that's it.

The Underwater River

Oh the ladies, who do they think they are
with their ceremony of slow inclinations,
whispering, "Really, I shouldn't," while smoothing
their latest devastating dress, or "It wouldn't be right,"
while brushing the wild languors of the moon
on a sculpted eyelid so when it's demurely lowered
it'll both desire and refuse us?

Who teaches them the degrees of radiant waiting,
the shadowy layers of no, saying, "How lovely, but
really I couldn't," as their fascist red nails
sail down and absently pull a hair back in place?
Oh, the ladies love to say no and then wait.

I love the way they vanish around corners or
shake out their hair in a flourish, or, smartly
crossing their legs beneath that haunted look
of being wanted, point their toe along an exact
thread of sexual tension, saying no without ever saying it.

Do they think they can fool us dogs when no means yes
and the back of their head seems a consummate invitation,
we who smell as if we've slept in our lives, who stand
like monolithic stones falling through vapor and breaking,
we who spend every moment watching and pretending not to notice?

We know about this, ladies, and in this dim-lit world
of artifice and ruin, if it came down to it,
each of us in his inmost secret heart knows
that if given the chance, he could've made a beautiful woman.

The Energy It Takes to Pass Through Solid Objects

for my son Jacob

My son with food on his face
is banging on his high chair like a prisoner
who has lost the ability to speak.

He would like to grab the cat
who has slipped by like the field mouse
fleeing her mind. His demands rise and disperse
like night rising off the skull of morning.

Last night we let him sleep between us
and he thrashed around wrestling sorrows
his own size. Then he sat up quietly
in the dark like a miniature alien,
my own exposed heart, calmly weighing
the critical mass of stillness between us.

My son with food on his face,
food oozing through his fists,
screams his life is like no other.
He is being pulled straight out of his chair
by the long black fur of his imagination
and all I can do, he screams, is nothing.

I try to remember but I can't sing
the song my mother sang to me
that made a solid object out of feeling.
I open my mouth and with the energy it takes
to pass through solid objects, I arrive silently
at that place from which all feeling comes.

It will take a long time to make him civil,
before we can unstrap him from the raucous
taste of peas and screaming orange carrots,
and let him leave this house. He will have to loop
on wider and wider journeys, joining his circle
to ours, until the food he orders is exotic,
and inside the elusive feel of soft black fur
is the woman he will marry and the raggle-taggle
parade of cats and family.

He cries and his cries float up, joining ours,
the ones we don't notice. So I show my son the rain
and he shrieks and shrieks delightedly.
This is how it is for him inside all day—
rain from one moment to the next, all day
falling down through wet hot exclamation points.

There is no toy for this. Only sleep.
And so I stay with him caught halfway in-between
the desire to be someone else and his stuffed animal,
mouth sewn shut, eyes pasted wide open, arms flung out.

I Don't Know, You Probably Know Everything I Know

for Walter Wetherell's bad back

Suddenly my leg goes numb, feels like
someone else's till the feeling comes back.
But it never feels as special
as when someone else is touching it.

It's the same way my hand feels
touching someone else; in other words,
my numb leg is to my hand touching it
as my hand feels touching someone else.

It's as if we were given someone else's hands
when we're the ones touching, and our own true hands
when we are being touched (you could substitute
"legs" for "hands" in the above), but I guess
if everything felt too good
then we'd never have any thoughts.

As you can see, I like thinking about what I don't
already know. What I already know feels numb,
like the hospital release form that says
it's okay with everyone if you end up paralyzed
since the brain your back connects can take over
the job of carrying whatever you have a mind to.

Just tell the surgeon when he cuts into your back
he could disconnect the sky from your fall and then
you wouldn't be able to touch anything at all;
not him, not you, not us. But I'm probably not
telling you anything you don't already know,
isn't that so?

Is that you, Walter?

The Stopover

Just as he was falling asleep, the phone rang.
It was a distant relative who had just "deplaned."
That word made it official, case closed, nothing could be done.

He looked up to heaven at his people from the Old Country
who wearily lifted their heads from shoveling six feet of snow
off the potato farm and asked as more snow fell,
"Has the time finally come when things have gone from bad to worse?"

Well, if she wanted to come, whoever she was,
then fine, she could come.
If it would bring a little happiness
into this sorry world,
then fine, let her come.

But first, business was bad.
And next, there was the shock
of going bald all at once.
And then there was a lifetime of
dwelling on death.
And now—what else?—this!
This just wasn't a good time for a visit.

A Living

for Jerry Stern

Jerry, you would've loved my grandmother's backyard.
Crabgrass, stickers, sand, rhubarb, and garbage cans
out of which leapt the Lords of Monday Morning—radiant
dog-size rats that I can still feel frisking the old
two-decker house from its stone-walled cellar
to its thin stink of whitefish in the upstairs kitchen.

We had a glowering skyline of houses back then that answered
the sea like Pop did the door: "Goddammit, who is it!?"
No lifeguards or pastel condos, just oceanfront property
like the kind you find on the Ganges, and pious old Jews
like Gramma Belle sitting in her picture window in a haze
of smoke and steaming coffee, staring at the waves of bygone years.

In those days no one got raped or robbed. The trend back then
was to drop dead in Miami, smelling of arguments, chicken soup,
and broken hallways. Am I coming through? All skin and bones
in my cheap gaberdines? Like we used to answer the question,
"So how are you?"—"So how should I be?"

I wasn't going to be another skinny Ashkenazi half-dead on the beach
from third-degree burns with a dumb newspaper boat on my head, afraid
of a heart attack in knee-deep water. So I stayed in the backyard
in the exotic green break of rhubarb, cracking a stalk in half,
sucking on the sour juice—Mr. Romance, who would one day score.

This morning my eyes are sore and there's a dark line down my cheek
like a near-death experience from a cello slide by Mahler.
I'm in my robe with its coffee stain like a monogram of my unconscious,
smoking, drinking coffee, walking to my classes at the university
to teach poetry, which can explain almost everything, and happens to be,
should someone like the landlord ask, a living.

Convention

Lately, all the letters I've received
have begun with *Dear Jack,*
followed by *I'm sorry* . . .
Someone is late or sad, or has been let down,
or needs me to enlist, needs a pal,
a pat on the back, a couple of bucks,
or insists he isn't clever enough.
Then the delicate exiting backward,
with the inscrutable *as ever*
blurred by the power surge
of an indelibly black signature,
a logo of panache and ruin.

Jane Goodall, who studied the convention
of contact in apes,
observed how it's expressed
in terms of psychophysical distance:
from cold ostracism
to the meticulous grooming of mates and pals
who'd just as soon chew a buddy's ear off
than offer him a bite.

Meanwhile, back in the twentieth century,
I'm posted here in the intersection
of canceled human traffic, spinning between
everyone's best intentions and their departing messes.
Yesterday I received a missive with a spot of
cat poo on it. The ammoniacal stench was circled,
with an arrow sharply drawn to it that said,
Blame the cat! I took this, in the larger sense,
as a signal of distress, the sender claiming
her territorial imperative to whatever kind
of human attention she could get.

People, I used to live for mail. I'd squat beside my
letter box idly pawing my granules of patience
like the exemplary Ms. Goodall who spent her life
diligently playing the monkey. Most of the primates
weren't fooled by this, except for one precocious ape
who half-heartedly tried to couple with Ms. Goodall,
but got stuck between maintaining his distance and
claiming boasting rights to what he thought
was the world's weirdest monkey.

It brought to mind what Keats always yelled at the women
in his flat: "Beauty is truth, truth, beauty,"
which I guess worked since things got quiet after that.
So, like that great Romantic I bathed in perfumed waters,
powdered, dressed up in my best jabot and velvet jacket,
and wrote: *Dear Whoever, Whatever, However, I'm sorry, As ever,*
then attacked my pile of correspondence
with the single-mindedness of a Xerox.

Woman in Translation

We made love once.
She took me to her place,
her bedroom with the maidenhair fern
delicately exploding in slow motion
over a naked window.

Maybe I was a little drunk
because I said I don't care
what time of month it is
and she said let me show you
my portfolio of sketches:

frame after frame of scissors
plunged through a field of deep white earth
then the tips of the scissors swirling down
into a rococo mass of roots and blood.

I think my mind held its breath
as I studied her clean execution
though I might've gasped,
though I might've closed my eyes
and courteously said yes.

Because then we made love
with the bed drenched in blood
and I found myself not feeling well,
saying no, no, and I can still hear her
asking, after I fled and slammed the door
ten years ago, "What . . . !?"

*

Somehow tonight I came across her again
on the cover of an art magazine.
She was really beautiful

in the black-and-white photo of her
with the tone drained
as if something overprocessed
had been fused to her face,
the eyes squinting a little at the viewer
as if she could not see—I heard
she turned gay and started a rock group—
a little crooked smile, a veiled look
like that window with a decision
exploded over it.

Or maybe this was a stand-in, some sister
she had invented to stand before the world,
someone with the look of erasure, as if
a calm "No" had sunk into her nerves,
and she was left to live
suspended in the solid air
between the one with the face of "No"
who was chosen to go through the world,
and the lost other one who stayed home
long after dark, bent over her work,
intensely creating the other.

What's the Difference?

After I've put it off
until my head fizzes
into a violent emptiness,
I let my hand crawl south
along my sleeping wife.

God knows where she is
in her sleep
or how far I'd have to travel
before my hand would dissolve
in equivocation. But

basically, she's a joyful person
who loves to make love in the light.

So I lay here fantasizing
I am my wife
who can't help
reaching for herself.

I've begun to adjust
to this unilateral
blinding of myself with lust,

not the least bit taken aback
with the knowledge that over the years
even the oddest-looking couples begin to look alike.

The Reception

for J. L.

She waited for me to enter,
then for me to see her.
I could tell by the long river of looking
she had me wade through, the same way
I had stared at the blue-green haze
of Boston Harbor, flying toward it for an hour,
not sure if I were looking at miles
of used-up air or cold salt water; the way
she shouted silently at me without pleasure,
her drink a hammer, throwing herself
through herself over and over, her head
numb against the wildly vibrating wall
of her impending separation.

I must have finally learned the trick
of thinking about a woman
without breaking my neck
because I blinked and smiled as if to say,
"I can't hear you above the din."
(I had gone through all this once and my own
children grew cold and formal and moved away.)
And I squinted into that held moment
so the noise of the celebratory room
could trickle in, burst, then flood over us.
And as she turned to leave,
bumping into others as if falling backward,
her eyes two weak lights bent down, searching
the dark road ahead, I suddenly remembered
what it's like to turn and have no home,
to have no home to go to,
to go home and turn
and have none.

Excuse Me

The average man has a sexual fantasy every ninety seconds
— item in *The Dallas Herald*

Somehow it seems noble to be obsessed
by thoughts of furthering one's race,
giving the body orders that you're not at home,
not to be disturbed. But I don't think
I'm one of these, I'm one of those
whose boorish little life is sporadically interrupted
by the surfacing of one long erotic subconscious thought
strung out like Morse code, and I'm stuck up here
faithfully transcribing the myopia of dots and dashes
wholly unaware of the unclean thoughts I'm reveling in
until one day a newspaper psychologist reveals to all
just what my other hand has apparently been doing.

Is anyone at home? Is anyone merely average?
Or are we just the pale cheese glued between
the wild extremes of Episcopalian kindness
and a bog-born rutting perversion,
doing next to nothing about our sex,
while a small handful of dedicated nympholeptics
make up the appalling difference?

On the other hand, maybe it's not our fault,
maybe it's the media's. On page sixteen of the paper
there's a full-page spread of Cher standing defiantly half-naked
like some bitch goddess of a healthy hi-tech universe,
with one arm cocked behind her neck,
her breasts peeking through a contemporary version
of medieval mail, a dumbbell hooked in the other,
suggestively flexed, saying,
"Excuses mean nothing to your thighs."
And I agree, though some of us may prefer our sex on page

eighteen where an ad for satin panties shows four quiescent nymphs
in their unmentionables, staring intensely from the page
as if they were watching something of special interest
slowly develop, like an idea, only physical.

Hey, I'd be the last one ever to be against thinking about sex
if I could help it. And I'm not even against basic sex itself—
Look, I'm here aren't I? I just want to be aware of my own
prurient interest and its improvisations, and not be under
the false impression I'm just enjoying a few risqué epiphanies
when in truth I'm dieseling out of my own terminal of smut
with people timing me and experts issuing exit polls.

Maybe it's because I've had to go so far out of myself
to appear normal that I always figured, hey, I must be exceptional
in some vague and funny way. But the average man never thinks
he's average—does he?— though if he were asked, I think he'd say
he spends most of his time just trying to get through the day.

Supersaver to Atlanta

Sitting next to me was a young black carpenter
who at the end of the trip, after several drinks
and nervous swappings of disorders and near disasters,
gently entrusted his name to me, "David."
Looking away, he told me about his six-year-old son
who didn't know his colors. "It hurt me," he said,
holding his hand against his heart, patting it,
then pointing at the sky full of continuing blue,
"that he'd look at this and guess it was red."
I felt bad for him, but thought that seeing blue
and saying red pointed to something basically true
about our nature.

"Where's he now?" I asked, fearing the worst,
flustered, as if I had spilled my drink in my lap.
"He's with my mother," he said. "I took him from my girl
who's too busy trying to look pretty for her men."
I asked if he were married and, without a trace of guilt,
he said, "No, she's got other kids by different men.
You got to put in time with kids. You got to pay
attention," he said, cupping his face against the window
so he could get a clearer view of what we were flying through.

He looked no older than my firstborn son
who lives away from me. He had a dark sweet face
but made sure he talked practical. Behind us
a squawky stewardess with a heavy Southern twang
kept going over and over the words for "right" and "left"
in Spanish: "Derecho. Derecho. A la izquierda." I thought
she had her genders switched but couldn't remember,
then realized she was practicing for a crash
and I settled on trying to memorize the exits.

Then he asked me if I'd like to play his *Word Games* book,
and I regret to say I told him I taught college English.
"Uh-huh, that's nice," he said, "that's nice . . ."
Then he opened up the book to the puzzle of *Cinderella*
whose camouflaged words ran forward, backward,
up and down, and obliquely within its square.
They were all there: <u>evening</u>, <u>sad</u>, <u>stepmother</u>, <u>prince</u>,
the story of the girl who suffered others' words
but paid attention and got her wish. Then I realized

if I just looked at the puzzle as if I were listening
to each individual instrument in a symphony all at once,
and honed in on the long horns floating in the middle,
that I could easily spot the word. I opened up my mind
and thought of Dick Hugo, the poet-bombardier who flew
thirty-five missions in a B-24 Liberator over Italy, his face
sucked tight against the gasket of the range finder,
exhausted to a zero. He ended up bombing Switzerland instead.
In the photo I have of him standing beside his crashed plane,
there's a crinkled drawing of Bugs Bunny on the fuselage,
asking "What's up Doc?"

Meanwhile David goes on telling me how God willed him
to Atlanta where he miraculously started his own business.
I closed my eyes and caught a sparkle off of Cinderella's
slipper, haloed in moonlight there on the dark stone steps,
then gave David back his book who easily circled the words
and explained with as much weight as words could carry
how marriage needed to fly in one direction, how he needed
a woman with ambition. Said he wasn't ready yet. I remembered
washing my face a few weeks back and looking in the mirror
and seeing my face distorted, pulled apart in five directions.
I thought finally I had glimpsed what I felt, saw

47

what I was feeling, until I realized that I was looking
into an empty paper towel dispenser that someone with good
reason, like me after my divorce, had smashed with his fist.

Now I was flying home to my new wife and kids, trying hard
to remember what I was like before I left. I wanted badly
to be what I was, if only for the family, if only for the sake
of making things smoother. David got up and was a lot shorter
than I had figured. He must've had very short legs because
through the whole trip we seemed eye-to-eye. Then he shook
my hand and quietly said his name and left. I wanted to say
that I'd write or call but I realized, really, we had nothing
at all in common, and as the surface of things took over,
people grabbing for their baggage, he melted into the line
of strangers who seemed so willing to live their lives like that.

Emerging from the walkway I caught my little son just as he
leapt flying into my arms and squealed and fervently
pressed his head against mine. Whoever I was I was home,
and I bent to kiss my wife on the lips and caught the whole
welcoming tribe of in-laws reverently lowering their heads,
and I carried my son against me for as long as I could like that.

Talking to Arthur

in memory of Arthur Feldman

I'm stuck here at a party listening to Arthur complain
that when you reach his age nobody knows anything.

He's telling me about his daughter who told him to go to hell,
mind his own business, which he explains he's retired from.

He's wearing a pair of those glaring state trooper sunglasses
that reflect the sun and make whoever you're talking to look tiny,

and I'm falling in line, lying to him to be nice,
telling him the older I get the less I seem to know.

He's gone from $180,000 a year onto Social Security,
got fired because he exposed his boss for taking bribes.

He goes on talking quietly about his ruin, half-hidden
by gusts of smoke from the barbecue, as if nobody's listening,

and then when he finally takes off his glasses and relaxes,
I see that filmy blue color old people get across their eyes

just before they die, and I feel I'm getting smaller and smaller
just as he wheels on me and says, "Whadda ya gonna do?"

Looking at Death Through Bad Eyes

All of a sudden his eyes went bad
and he had to wear an ugly old pair
of old-fogey bifocals.
So he bought the glasses and began training himself:
which lens to look through at which time,
how to balance the glasses on top of his head to look busy,
how to stick them on the end of his nose to appear intense,
how to expertly flip them open when a decision had to be reached,
how to click them shut when a decision had been made,
how to hold them like a teacup when he wanted to appear pleasant,
how to suck seductively on them when he had nothing at all in mind,
how to hold them up and examine the skies for a spot,
how to clean the smudges that got all over them from his face,
and how to appear ruthless or kind or wonderful and wise
or dreamy or nervous or pompous and brutish; in short, that year,
in the middle of making himself an expert at wearing glasses,
he died.

The One in Which

He thinks that I'm a sailor,
But knows I have no ship.
And that we have no sea.
Only vast distances, and winds.
                —Yehuda Amichai, *"My Child"*

He gets up
all hours of the night
capriciously crying
"It's daylight! Daylight!"
like some mad watchman
wearing a helmet of fog
for the life in which
he streams through dreaming,
a helmet of light
for the one in which
he stumbles into being.

Floating here
in the king-size darkness
of our bed,
he has a few great things
to do,
and with his little finger,
acute as any cry, he points
to something far away,
and we hug each other
going there,
my little General of Surprise
and me, his obedient attaché,
relieved to think
at least we have our orders.

Please, Not All at Once

I've left markers
in places where
I've left off
reading every book
in the house,
places where
my own stray thoughts
must've overpowered me,
or what I was reading,
or wished I had said,
or maybe someone
finally got through
to me. Wouldn't it be nice
if I got up now
and checked out
all those places
where I stopped
just to see if
they were all the same
word, or ended in the
beginning of some belief
or grief, or worse,
they were all different
and it all meant nothing
like letting the cat out
just as a car bomb
goes off in Beirut
on my unplugged TV?
After forty-five years of
investigations broken
off and loaded questions,
I still don't know

if I'm complex or just
above being stupid
or if at different times
I'm both. And I don't want
an answer to this but
I ask you is it or is it not
more than enough
just to know when to stop?

From the Luxury Condo on the Sea

For three days there's been a ship
anchored in the harbor
like a word said
quietly and truly in the dark,
a word you can't take back
from the vast embattled silence
sealed by gray sky and water.

A small plume of smoke
smudges off the stern
against the steel-colored dawn
giving it the feel of a muted
Japanese scroll.
Or maybe it's on fire.

I fit my face to the binoculars,
eyes strafing, godlike,
speeding out closer, fine-tuning
the water that shivers like a mirror
chilled by flying through time.

Heavy industry, floating.
I don't know how to read the dark
mechanisms of stacks and catwalks
which, oddly, resemble a shipyard at sea,
or a prehistoric crustacean on its back,
except to imagine its insides are filled
with oil—trees and animals 100,000 years old.

Dwarfed by comparison,
off to the right,
is a small wooden lobster boat
sliding slowly in a half-circle,
like the pleasure of music,

smoothing out the water
it was made to endure.

There's a man leaning over the gunnels
hauling up dripping cages,
shredding the side of the boat
into ribbons of light
as I did once,
pulling up the writhing treasure
of mechanical black lobsters
and sometimes a shark,
like the realization of being
far out at sea
suddenly brought on board.

Out there beyond the twelve-mile limit
Russian trawlers are dragging lobsters
into steel cages the size of this room.
That's why I couldn't feed my family
and mostly took the kids for rides.

I thought there must be a way
to study the life of *Homarus americanus*
who seemed to crawl aimlessly
across the ocean floor
under the tonnage of darkness.
It must seek purpose through order
as we do and if I could determine this
then I'd be a success.

I think I gave the boat away
for the memory of floating
on those glassy August mornings,
which wasn't the first time I left

♪♪

something just when something had to be done
and ended up doing something else.

But I love this world and the way one thing
becomes another, how the impossible is pitted
against the hoping against the odds,
the freighter smoking, warming up, the man
bent over half-disappearing into the sea,

the one high up putting the binoculars down
and stretching with a whole long day of nothing to do
before him, who even with the power of recall
and binoculars can't understand the difference
between here and there, now and then,

and the lobsters in their gorgeous black armor
tippling across the darkness, their eyes swiveling,
standing out on stalks, the world bearing down
and slowly moving by them with their delicate,
finely ringed antennae waving.

I'm great, 100%, when I'm left alone
and I don't have anything to do
or have to be anything for anyone,
and no one is measuring just how little
or maladjusted I've become.

But the minute I meet humans
things get tragic.
I must have the gift to connect
right into their main switchbox
because as soon as we start kibitzing
the masks light up, the lies flicker
and ding and go bong, and the score
reaches into the billions.

It reminds me of those times
I barely lived through
when someone woke up and decided
to make a god out of Pee-Wee Herman,
and there were just a few of us left
who stayed put in our rooms during this
and then later just as I get over this
there's a conspiracy to bring back the 1950s.

So whoever it is I'm talking to
I'm just passing the time, the age,
but inside I'm burning to the ground
with this anguished expression of horror
slowly developing like a Polaroid
on my face, and we're both sort of
watching this until I break it off
by screaming "Taxi!" and I get in
and the cabby throws the meter
and I can hear him telling himself

over the radio just how he's gonna
screw me . . . Am I at some stage in my life
that nobody talks about,
something akin to how wild animals
can smell a woman's period a mile off?

The only times the wires aren't crossed
are like when I took my cat to the vet
and asked the receptionist with latex gloves
in the glassed-in booth
with the mouth-size hole in it
how much it was gonna cost
for my cat's eighth batch of kittens
and she said, "For crissakes, fella,
whydonchagetitfixed!?"

One, Two, Three, Four, Five . . .

It was when I became pubescent that I developed
a bad attitude.
They said we'll have to amputate,
do you want to watch or be knocked out,
are you a man or a mouse?

The nurse who was good-looking was hoping
I'd choose number one.
She wore a white mask, white cap,
white uniform, and gauze bandages on her feet.
She never talked or blinked
and I loved her for that.
I'm almost certain she was a woman.

I counted thousands of seconds in my head
and then looked over and checked myself
against the unmoving operating room clock.
I was never more than a few seconds off.
I was never more than a few seconds off.

Nothing Else

I must've been fifteen at the time
because as I'm remembering this
the same egregious feeling is beginning
to crawl through my fingertips
just itching to get back at the wheel.
But there I am all dressed up,
crammed into the backseat with the dark
and lovely Rita who, rumor had it,
would give you a feel if and when
she felt like it. And I made sure
in my sly, shy way with a particularly
suggestive orchid I pinned to her
that she did.

I don't know who was in the backseat with us
or who was driving, but we were on our way back
from dancing the Apple Jack
to Bill Haley and the Comets, live,
and I remember the luxurious feeling of her silk blouse
falling open in the dark.
I softly pushed her bra aside
and just sort of weighed them for a while.
Then I sculpted and smoothed, rounded and brooded
over them so that forever after my mind's circuitry
could flash the afterimage of them.
Rita just sort of closed her eyes and smiled.
She seemed all feeling. But she must've been thinking
of someone else since that's the last time I'd ever see her.

She knew there'd be other girls who'd bring me along,
that next year I'd do 120 in my dad's convertible,
two tons of steel hurtling down an empty route,

barely touching the ground, the top ballooning
like a shout, its ecstatic grillwork lit up and grinning
like my adolescent face. That was the first and last time
I closed my eyes and thought that nothing but myself could catch me,
my licensed hands frozen to the wheel so hard I couldn't feel them.

The Bam Butti: Pygmies of the Congo

This morning my woman is pulling every leaf from our hut
and is threatening to walk off to her mother's. If I stop her
in time with an apology, she will peek at me and smile and say
she has decided to take our hut down, leaf by leaf, to wash it
in the river. To us, an act performed correctly can keep death away.

We know that women own the fires of birth and death, and that men
own the shadows of things seen in daylight. That is why we start in
with our big noise about what it is to be a man and drink too many cups of
wine and boast of how we have slept with all the sweet banana girls.
There has always been much rain and much looking at rain from our huts.

For a man to be a man he must get up early one day, kick down his house,
rub ashes into the fresh cuts on his forehead, and decide to kill something
big. But for a woman, one day her breasts sprout, the moon comes down
to sleep with her, and soon she has the flow of blood and can make life.
She circles her face and breasts and buttocks with fruit paste,
puts on her powerful leaf skirt, and with the old singing and dancing
starts to hunt her man.

We men feel the way a sleeper feels when a dream is running through him.
Sometimes one of us gets brave and takes three wives into a tree.
But this is like the children's game of the snapping tree.
Everyone laughs and piles on but when the tree snaps back
he is alone in the sky and there is an end to happiness.

When the honey season ends, we blow the long molino horn which is
longer than five men and makes the sound of smoke falling through us.
It tells us we cannot see our lives which are like our
deepest dreams which change into spirits who can outrun us.

We send the echo of the horn onto the top of the world because
our echoes are the dream of what we say, like smoke and rain,
and because whoever owns the world and whoever made us must
    want to know
that the BamButti are happy and that we are still well made.

For most of the facts poeticized here, and for some phrasing, I am indebted to
Colin M. Turnbull's beautiful work, *The Forest People: A Study of the Pygmies
of the Congo* (New York: Simon and Schuster, 1961).

About the Author

JACK MYERS, co-editor of *New American Poets of the '90s* (Godine, 1991), is the author of six volumes of poetry and five other works about poetry. His collection *As Long as You're Happy* was the National Poetry Series selection for 1985. Most recently, he co-edited *A Profile of Twentieth-Century American Poetry* with David Wojahn. Born in Massachusetts, Jack Myers teaches at Southern Methodist University and Vermont College.

Colophon

Blindsided was designed by Scott-Martin Kosofsky at the Philidor Company in Boston. The text typeface is Montaigne Sabon, designed and made by Mr. Kosofsky, based on the work of Jan Tschichold. The titles are set in Pepita, one of Imre Reiner's most lively scripts, originally produced for metal-casting by the Monotype Corporation in 1957.

The book was entirely produced on the Macintosh. The pages were composed in QuarkXpress; the decorative elements in Adobe Illustrator; and the cover in Adobe Photoshop.

The film was produced by Aurora Graphics of Portsmouth, New Hampshire. The book was printed and bound by Haddon Craftsmen, Scranton, Pennsylvania.